Next in Line: Navigating the World of Replaceability in Business

Dr. Jose A. Mendez

Published by Christian Cross Publishing LLC, 2024.

While every precaution has been taken in the preparation of this book, the publisher assumes no responsibility for errors or omissions, or for damages resulting from the use of the information contained herein.

NEXT IN LINE: NAVIGATING THE WORLD OF REPLACEABILITY IN BUSINESS

First edition. March 1, 2024.

ISBN: 979-8224195411

Written by Dr. Jose A. Mendez.

Also by Dr. Jose A. Mendez

Warrior Mindset: A Veteran's Guide to Entrepreneurship and Business
Next in Line: Navigating the World of Replaceability in Business

Table of Contents

Dedication

I would like to extend my heartfelt gratitude to Zack "Gibby" Gibson, the red barber, for the enlightening conversation we shared. Your perspective on the notion that everyone is replaceable sparked a profound contemplation within me, igniting a fire of inspiration.

Your suggestion to pen a business book on this very topic was not only insightful but also timely. In a world where the dynamics of business and employment are constantly evolving, the concept of replaceability holds immense significance. Your sagacity and conversations have provided me with a fresh lens on an amazing topic to explore and elucidate on this crucial aspect of organizational dynamics.

I am deeply appreciative of the time and thoughts you generously shared during our interactions. Our conversation has set me on a path towards creating a meaningful contribution to the discourse surrounding business and human resources.

Once again, thank you, Zack "Gibby" Gibson, for your invaluable input in our discussion. This book is because of you.

ACKNOWLEDGMENTS

TO MY DEAREST WIFE,

As I sit down to write these words of acknowledgment, I am overwhelmed with gratitude for the unwavering support, love, and inspiration you have showered upon me throughout the journey of writing this book.

Your patience during the long hours I spent lost in thought, your encouragement when doubts clouded my mind, and your belief in my abilities even when I faltered have been the cornerstone of my strength. Your unwavering faith in me has been a beacon of light guiding me through the darkest of moments.

Your understanding and willingness to sacrifice your time and attention so that I could pursue my passion have not gone unnoticed. Your selflessness and dedication to our family have been the driving force behind my determination to succeed.

This book is not just a product of my efforts but a testament to the love and support of an extraordinary woman. Your presence in my life has enriched it in ways I could never have imagined, and for that, I am eternally grateful.

Thank you for being my rock, my muse, and my partner in every sense of the word. I dedicate this book to you, my beloved wife, with all my heart.

With all my love,

Chapter 1: The Myth of Indispensability

The Fallacy of Job Security

In the world of business, there is a pervasive fallacy that many individuals hold onto dearly - the idea of job security. People often believe that if they work hard, meet their targets, and stay loyal to their company, they will have a secure job for life. However, this belief is nothing more than a myth that can lead to complacency and stagnation in one's career. Long gone are the day where people worked for and retired from one company.

The truth is, in today's business landscape, no one is truly immune to being replaced. Companies are constantly evolving, adapting to new technologies, and looking for ways to increase efficiency and profitability. This means that even the most dedicated and hardworking employees can find themselves out of a job if they are no longer seen as essential to the organization.

The fallacy of job security can be particularly harmful to individuals who become too comfortable in their roles and stop striving for growth and improvement. Instead of resting on your laurels and assuming that your job is safe, it is important to continually assess your skills, knowledge, and performance to ensure that you remain relevant and valuable to your employer.

For business people, entrepreneurs, managers, and the general public, it is crucial to understand that everyone is replaceable in the business world. This realization can be a powerful motivator to stay on top of your game, constantly seeking new opportunities for growth and development, and being open to change and adaptation.

By embracing the idea that job security is a fallacy, individuals can position themselves as indispensable assets to their organizations, ready to navigate the ever-evolving world of business with confidence and agility.

The Evolution of Business Dynamics

In today's business world, the only constant is change. The evolution of business dynamics has been shaped by various factors, including technological advancements, globalization, and shifting consumer preferences. As a result, businesses must adapt and innovate in order to stay competitive and relevant in the ever-changing market.

One key aspect of the evolution of business dynamics is the concept that everyone is replaceable. In the past, businesses relied heavily on key individuals for their success. However, in today's digitally interconnected and fast-moving world, no one person is indispensable. This shift in mindset has led to a more dynamic and flexible approach to business operations.

The rise of automation and artificial intelligence has also played a significant role in changing the way businesses operate. Many routine tasks that were once performed by humans can now be automated, freeing up time and resources for more strategic initiatives. This has led to a greater focus on innovation and creativity in the business world.

Another important aspect of the evolution of business dynamics is the increasing importance of data and analytics. Businesses are now able to collect and analyze vast amounts of data to gain insights into consumer behavior and market trends. This data-driven approach has revolutionized the way businesses make decisions and develop strategies.

Overall, the evolution of business dynamics has led to a more competitive business environment. Businesses must be agile, innovative, and adaptable in order to succeed in this ever-changing landscape. By embracing change and staying ahead of the curve, businesses can position themselves for long-term success in the dynamic world of replaceability.

Embracing Change and Adaptability

In business, one thing is certain - change is inevitable. Whether it's advancements in technology, shifts in consumer preferences, or economic fluctuations, the only constant is change. As such, it is crucial for individuals in the business world to embrace change and cultivate adaptability in order to thrive in today's competitive landscape.

Embracing change means being open to new ideas, technologies, and ways of doing things. It requires a willingness to step out of your comfort zone and try new approaches, even if they may seem daunting at first. By embracing change, you can position yourself as a forward-thinker in your industry, staying ahead of the curve and seizing new opportunities as they arise.

Adaptability is another key trait that successful business people possess. Being adaptable means being able to pivot and adjust quickly in response to changing circumstances. It requires a nimble mindset and a willingness to learn and grow from every experience. Those who are adaptable are able to weather storms, navigate challenges, and emerge stronger on the other side.

In this book, readers will learn the importance of embracing change and adaptability in order to stay relevant and competitive in today's business world. Through examples, practical tips, and insightful strategies, this book will equip business people, entrepreneurs, managers, and the general public with the tools they need to thrive in an ever-evolving marketplace.

Remember, in the world of business, everyone is replaceable. Those who embrace change and cultivate adaptability are the ones who will rise to the top and secure their place in the future of business.

Chapter 2: Understanding the Concept of Replaceability

Defining Replaceability in Business

In business, the concept of replaceability is a crucial one that all individuals must understand in order to thrive and succeed in their careers. Defining replaceability in business is essential for individuals to recognize their value and contributions to their organizations, as well as to understand the importance of being adaptable and continuously improving their skills.

Replaceability in business refers to the idea that every individual within an organization has the potential to be replaced by someone else who possesses similar skills, knowledge, and experience. This concept may seem daunting at first, but it is important to remember that it is not a reflection of one's worth as a person or professional. Rather, it is a reality of the competitive business world in which we live.

For business people, entrepreneurs, managers, and the general public, understanding replaceability can serve as a motivator to continuously strive for excellence and to stay ahead of the curve in terms of skills and knowledge. By recognizing that they are replaceable, individuals can take proactive steps to ensure that they are always in demand and valuable to their organizations.

In the world of "Everyone is Replaceable," individuals must focus on honing their unique skills and abilities, building strong relationships with colleagues and clients, and staying up-to-date on industry trends and developments. By doing so, individuals can position themselves as indispensable assets to their organizations, making themselves less replaceable and more valuable in the eyes of their employers.

Defining replaceability in business is essential for individuals to understand their role within their organizations and to take proactive steps to ensure their long-term success. By recognizing the importance of staying ahead of the curve and continuously improving their skills, individuals can thrive in the competitive world of business and position themselves as invaluable assets to their organizations.

Identifying Key Factors for Replaceability

The concept of replaceability is a key factor that can greatly impact the success of a company. Identifying key factors for replaceability is essential for ensuring that the right people are in the right positions within an organization. This section we will delve into the various factors that contribute to replaceability and how they can be identified and managed effectively.

One of the key factors for replaceability is skillset. It is important for individuals within an organization to possess the necessary skills and expertise to effectively perform their roles. Identifying the specific skills that are required for each position can help ensure that the right people are in place to drive the success of the business.

Another important factor is attitude and work ethic. Individuals who possess a positive attitude, strong work ethic, and a willingness to learn and grow are more likely to be successful in their roles. Identifying individuals with the right attitude can help ensure that they are able to adapt to changing circumstances and continue to perform effectively in their positions.

Additionally, cultural fit is an important factor for replaceability. Individuals who align with the values, mission, and goals of the organization are more likely to thrive in their roles and contribute to the overall success of the business. Identifying individuals who are a good cultural fit can help ensure that they are able to integrate seamlessly into the organization and work well with others.

Overall, identifying key factors for replaceability is essential for ensuring that the right people are in the right positions within an organization. By focusing on skillset, attitude, work ethic, and cultural fit, businesses can effectively manage replaceability and set themselves up for long-term success.

Assessing Your Own Replaceability Quotient

In business, it is crucial to understand your own replaceability quotient. This concept refers to how easily you could be replaced within your organization or industry. By assessing your own replaceability quotient, you can take proactive steps to ensure your value and relevance in the workplace.

To begin assessing your replaceability quotient, consider your skill set and expertise. Are there others within your organization who possess similar skills and knowledge? If so, what sets you apart from them? Identify your unique strengths and capabilities that make you an invaluable asset to your team.

Next, evaluate your performance and contributions to the organization. Have you consistently exceeded expectations and delivered exceptional results? Do you bring innovative ideas and solutions to the table? Reflect on how your work has made a positive impact on the company and consider ways to further enhance your value.

It is also important to assess your adaptability and willingness to learn. In a changing business landscape, those who are open to acquiring new skills and knowledge are more likely to stay ahead of the curve. Stay curious, seek out opportunities for growth, and demonstrate your ability to evolve with the demands of the industry.

Ultimately, understanding your replaceability quotient requires a combination of self-awareness, continuous improvement, and strategic thinking. By taking proactive steps to enhance your skills, performance, and adaptability, you can increase your value within the organization and position yourself as an indispensable asset in the world of business.

Remember, everyone is replaceable to some extent. However, by assessing and improving your own replaceability quotient, you can increase your chances of standing out and thriving in a competitive business environment.

Chapter 3: The Consequences of Ignoring Replaceability

Stagnation and Obsolescence

Stagnation and obsolescence are two major threats that can hinder the success of any business or individual in the competitive landscape of today's business world. Staying stagnant is equivalent to falling behind. Therefore, it is crucial for business people, entrepreneurs, managers, and the general public to understand the implications of stagnation and obsolescence in order to stay relevant and competitive.

Stagnation occurs when individuals or businesses become complacent with their current position and fail to adapt to changing market trends and technologies. This can lead to a decline in productivity, innovation, and ultimately, profitability. On the other hand, obsolescence occurs when a person or a business becomes outdated and irrelevant due to advancements in technology, changes in consumer preferences, or shifts in the industry landscape.

In today's business environment, where everyone is replaceable, it is essential to continuously innovate, adapt, and reinvent oneself to stay ahead of the curve. This involves embracing change, seeking out opportunities for growth, and being open to new ideas and perspectives. By doing so, individuals and businesses can avoid the pitfalls of stagnation and obsolescence and remain competitive in their respective fields.

Ultimately, the key to overcoming stagnation and obsolescence lies in a willingness to learn, evolve, and take calculated risks. By staying proactive, agile, and forward-thinking, individuals and businesses can position themselves as leaders in their industries and ensure long-term success. So, remember, in the world where everyone is replaceable, staying relevant is the key to staying ahead.

Missed Opportunities for Growth

Missed opportunities for growth can be detrimental to both individuals and companies as a whole. In this book, the concept of missed opportunities for growth is explored in depth, shedding light on the importance of seizing every chance for advancement and development.

For business people, entrepreneurs, managers, and the general public, understanding the impact of missed opportunities for growth is crucial. Whether it is a missed chance to expand into a new market, improve a product or service, or develop a new skill set, these missed opportunities can hinder progress and success. In a world where everyone is replaceable, failing to capitalize on opportunities for growth can result in falling behind the competition and ultimately being replaced.

One common reason for missed opportunities for growth is complacency. When individuals or companies become comfortable with the status quo, they may overlook potential avenues for improvement and expansion. It is essential to constantly evaluate and reassess current strategies and practices to identify areas for growth and development.

Another reason for missed opportunities for growth is fear of failure. Many individuals and companies are hesitant to take risks or step out of their comfort zones for fear of making mistakes. However, it is often through taking calculated risks and learning from failures that the greatest opportunities for growth arise.

In "Next in Line," readers are encouraged to embrace change, take risks, and seize every opportunity for growth that comes their way. By being proactive, adaptable, and open to new possibilities, individuals and companies can position themselves for success and avoid being replaced in an ever-evolving business landscape. Remember, in a world where everyone is replaceable, missed opportunities for growth can be the difference between staying ahead of the curve or being left behind.

Impact on Team Dynamics and Company Culture

Team dynamics and company culture play a crucial role in the success and longevity of any organization. When a key member of a team is replaced, whether by choice or necessity, the impact on team dynamics and company culture can be profound.

One of the immediate effects of a team member being replaced is the disruption it can cause to the existing team dynamic. Each member of a team brings their own unique skills, personality, and way of working to the table. When someone new is brought in to replace a departing team member, it can take time for the team to adjust to this change. This adjustment period can lead to friction, misunderstandings, and a decrease in overall team morale.

Additionally, the replacement of a team member can also have a ripple effect on company culture. Company culture is the shared values, beliefs, and behaviors that define an organization and its employees. When a key team member is replaced, it can disrupt the established norms and routines that make up the company culture. This can lead to uncertainty, anxiety, and a sense of instability among the remaining team members.

However, it is important to remember that change is a natural part of business, and with the right approach, the impact on team dynamics and company culture can be managed effectively. Clear communication, transparency, and support from leadership are key to helping the team navigate through this period of transition. By fostering open dialogue, setting clear expectations, and providing resources for team members to adjust to the change, a company can minimize the negative impact on team dynamics and company culture.

Remember, everyone is replaceable. However, by proactively addressing the impact of team changes on dynamics and culture, organizations can ensure a smooth transition and maintain a positive and productive work environment for all employees.

Chapter 4: The Illusion of Job Security

Dissecting the Concept of Job Security

In today's society and working culture, the concept of job security has become increasingly elusive. The traditional notion of a stable, lifelong career with a single employer is no longer the norm. Instead, employees are constantly faced with the threat of being replaced by technology, automation, or outsourcing.

In this subchapter, we will dissect the concept of job security and explore why the idea of being irreplaceable in the workplace is no longer realistic. We will examine the factors that contribute to job insecurity, such as advancements in technology, global competition, and shifting market demands.

One of the key insights we will explore is the idea that everyone is replaceable in the business world. With the rise of artificial intelligence and machine learning, many routine tasks that were once performed by humans can now be automated. This means that even highly skilled professionals are at risk of being replaced by machines.

For business people, entrepreneurs, managers, and the general public, understanding the concept of job security is crucial for navigating the modern workplace. By recognizing that no job is completely secure, individuals can take proactive steps to future-proof their careers. This may involve acquiring new skills, staying abreast of industry trends, and continuously evolving as a professional.

Ultimately, the key to surviving in a world where everyone is replaceable is to embrace change and adaptability. By remaining flexible and open to new opportunities, individuals can position themselves for success in an ever-evolving business environment.

Common misconceptions about loyalty and longevity

Common misconceptions about loyalty and longevity can often lead to unrealistic expectations and disappointments in the business world. In the competitive business landscape of today, it is essential to debunk these myths and focus on strategies that will drive success and growth.

One common misconception is that loyalty equates to longevity in a company. While it is true that loyal employees can be valuable assets, it is important to remember that loyalty alone does not guarantee job security. In a world where businesses are constantly evolving and adapting to change, employees must also demonstrate their value through their skills, performance, and ability to contribute to the organization's goals.

Another misconception is that longevity in a company automatically translates to success. While long-serving employees may have valuable knowledge and experience, it is essential to recognize that innovation and adaptation are critical for long-term success. Businesses that fail to evolve and embrace change risk becoming obsolete.

Furthermore, the belief that certain positions are irreplaceable can hinder growth and innovation within an organization. Every employee, regardless of their role, should be encouraged to continuously improve their skills, seek new opportunities for growth, and contribute to the overall success of the company.

By understanding and debunking these common misconceptions about loyalty and longevity, business people, entrepreneurs, managers, and the general public can better navigate the world of replaceability in business. Embracing change, fostering innovation, and valuing the contributions of all employees are key to driving success and staying ahead in today's competitive market.

Impact of Technological Advancements on Job Stability

In today's rapidly evolving technological landscape, the impact of advancements on job stability is a pressing concern for business people, entrepreneurs, managers, and the general public. The rise of automation, artificial intelligence, and other disruptive technologies has revolutionized the way we work, presenting both opportunities and challenges for individuals in the workforce.

One of the key implications of technological advancements is the potential for job displacement. As machines become more capable of performing tasks traditionally done by humans, the need for human labor in certain industries may decrease. This can lead to job losses and increased competition for remaining positions, putting pressure on individuals to upskill and adapt to changing job requirements.

Furthermore, the rise of the gig economy and remote work has also changed the traditional employment landscape. Many companies are now relying on freelancers, contractors, and remote workers to fill roles that were once held by full-time employees. This shift towards a more flexible workforce can create uncertainty for individuals seeking long-term job stability.

However, technological advancements also bring opportunities for innovation and growth. Businesses that embrace automation and digital transformation can increase efficiency, reduce costs, and deliver better products and services to customers. By leveraging technology to streamline processes and improve productivity, companies can create new job opportunities and drive economic growth.

The impact of technological advancements on job stability is a complex and multifaceted issue that requires careful consideration. While advancements in technology have the potential to disrupt traditional job roles, they also offer opportunities for individuals and businesses to thrive in an increasingly digital world. By staying informed, adaptable, and proactive in response to technological change, individuals can position themselves for success in the evolving job market.

Chapter 5: Strategies for Navigating Replaceability

Developing a Growth Mindset

In the competitive world of business, it is essential to adopt a growth mindset in order to stay ahead of the curve and remain relevant in your industry. Developing a growth mindset is crucial for business people, entrepreneurs, managers, and the general public, especially in a world where the mantra of "everyone is replaceable" is becoming increasingly prevalent.

A growth mindset is the belief that one's abilities and intelligence can be developed through hard work, dedication, and perseverance. Those with a growth mindset are more likely to embrace challenges, learn from feedback, and see failures as opportunities for growth. This mindset is essential for navigating the world of replaceability in business, as it allows individuals to adapt to new technologies, trends, and market demands.

To develop a growth mindset, it is important to cultivate a passion for learning and improvement. This can be done through seeking out new opportunities for growth, setting ambitious goals, and challenging oneself to step outside of their comfort zone. It is also important to surround oneself with like-minded individuals who can provide support, encouragement, and feedback.

In a world where everyone is replaceable, those with a growth mindset are better equipped to stay ahead of the competition and remain relevant in their industry. By continuously seeking out new challenges, learning from failures, and adapting to change, individuals can position themselves as valuable assets in the ever-evolving world of business.

By developing a growth mindset, business people, entrepreneurs, managers, and the general public can not only survive in a world where everyone is replaceable but thrive and excel in their respective fields. Embracing a growth mindset is the key to staying relevant, competitive, and indispensable in business.

Building Transferable Skills

It is essential to continuously develop and hone skills that are transferable across various roles and industries. Building transferable skills not only makes you more adaptable and versatile in your career, but also increases your value as an employee. For employees it's indispensable cultivating these skills and understanding how they can help you stay ahead in the ever-changing business landscape.

One of the key benefits of transferable skills is the ability to seamlessly transition between different roles or industries. As the saying goes, "everyone is replaceable," so it is crucial to have a diverse set of skills that can be applied in a variety of situations. By investing time and effort into developing transferable skills such as communication, problem-solving, and leadership, you can ensure that you are always in demand and prepared for whatever challenges come your way.

Additionally, building transferable skills can also lead to increased job satisfaction and career growth. Employers value employees who have a wide range of skills and are able to adapt to different environments, making you a valuable asset to any organization. By continuously expanding your skillset, you open yourself up to new opportunities for advancement and personal development.

Whether you are a business person, entrepreneur, manager, or simply a member of the general public looking to enhance your career prospects, building transferable skills is essential in today's competitive job market. "Next in Line" provides valuable insights and practical tips on how you can develop these skills and thrive in a world where everyone is replaceable. Take charge of your career and invest in yourself – the possibilities are endless when you have a strong foundation of transferable skills.

Cultivating a Strong Personal Brand

Cultivating a strong personal brand is more important now than ever, and the significance of building a personal brand that sets you apart from the crowd and helps you stand out in a sea of replaceable individuals cannot be ignored.

For business people, entrepreneurs, managers, and the general public, understanding the value of a strong personal brand is crucial for success. Your personal brand is what differentiates you from others and showcases your unique skills, experiences, and values. It is what makes you memorable and desirable to potential employers, clients, and partners.

In a world where everyone is replaceable, a strong personal brand can be your secret weapon. By cultivating a brand that authentically represents who you are and what you stand for, you can attract opportunities that align with your goals and values. Whether you are looking to advance in your career, start your own business, or simply stand out in your industry, a strong personal brand can help you achieve your objectives.

In "Next in Line," we provide practical tips and strategies for building a personal brand that resonates with your target audience and sets you apart from the competition. From defining your unique value proposition to leveraging social media and networking opportunities, this book offers actionable advice for cultivating a strong personal brand that serves as a powerful asset in a competitive business landscape.

Don't get lost in the crowd of replaceable individuals. Cultivate a strong personal brand that showcases your unique talents and strengths, and watch as opportunities come knocking at your door. Your personal brand is your most valuable asset – invest in it wisely.

Chapter 6: The Value of Adaptability

Traits of an Adaptable Employee

One of the most valuable traits an employee can possess is adaptability. Adaptability is a key characteristic that make an employee adaptable and indispensable in today's ever-changing work environment.

One of the most important traits of an adaptable employee is a willingness to learn and grow. This means being open to new ideas, technologies, and ways of working. Adaptable employees are constantly seeking out opportunities for professional development and are not afraid to step out of their comfort zones to try new things.

Another essential trait of an adaptable employee is resilience. In a world where change is constant, it's important to be able to bounce back from setbacks and challenges. Adaptable employees are able to stay positive and focused even in the face of adversity, using each experience as an opportunity to learn and improve.

Flexibility is also a key trait of an adaptable employee. This means being able to adjust to new situations quickly and effectively, whether it's a change in project scope, team dynamics, or work environment. Adaptable employees are able to pivot and adapt their approach to meet the needs of the business and their colleagues.

Finally, communication skills are crucial for an adaptable employee. Being able to effectively communicate with colleagues, managers, and clients is essential for navigating the complexities of the modern workplace. Adaptable employees are able to listen actively, express their ideas clearly, and collaborate effectively with others.

Overall, the traits of an adaptable employee are essential for success. By cultivating these characteristics, employees can position themselves as indispensable assets to their organizations, ensuring their continued success and growth in the future.

Strategies for Fostering Adaptability within Organizations

In a rapidly changing business landscape, adaptability is key to survival and success. Organizations that are able to quickly pivot and adjust to new challenges are more likely to thrive in an ever-evolving market. In this subchapter, we will explore strategies for fostering adaptability within organizations.

One of the most important strategies for fostering adaptability is to create a culture that values innovation and flexibility. This starts at the top, with leaders who are willing to embrace change and encourage their teams to think outside the box. By fostering a culture of experimentation and risk-taking, organizations can create an environment where employees feel empowered to adapt to new challenges.

Another key strategy for fostering adaptability is to invest in continuous learning and development. By providing employees with the tools and resources they need to stay current in their field, organizations can ensure that their teams are equipped to adapt to new technologies and trends. This can include offering training programs, workshops, and mentorship opportunities, as well as encouraging employees to pursue ongoing education and certifications.

Additionally, organizations can foster adaptability by promoting collaboration and communication among team members. By creating cross-functional teams and encouraging employees to work together on projects, organizations can break down silos and promote a culture of information sharing. This can help teams adapt more quickly to new challenges and find creative solutions to complex problems.

Overall, fostering adaptability within organizations requires a combination of leadership support, continuous learning, and collaboration. By implementing these strategies, organizations can position themselves for success in an ever-changing business landscape.

How Adaptability Mitigates the Fear of Being Replaced

Fear of being replaced is a common concern for many employees. However, there is a way to mitigate this fear and ensure that you remain valuable to your organization - adaptability.

Adaptability is the ability to adjust to new conditions and changes in the workplace. By being adaptable, you can demonstrate your willingness to learn new skills, take on new challenges, and embrace change. This not only makes you a more valuable asset to your organization but also reduces the likelihood of being replaced.

One of the key ways that adaptability can help mitigate the fear of being replaced is by making you more versatile. When you are adaptable, you are able to take on a variety of tasks and roles within the organization. This makes you indispensable, as you can easily transition between different projects and responsibilities as needed.

Additionally, being adaptable can help you stay ahead of the curve in an ever-evolving business landscape. By continuously learning and growing, you can position yourself as a valuable resource to your organization, making it less likely that you will be replaced.

Furthermore, adaptability can help you build resilience in the face of change. Instead of being fearful of being replaced, you can embrace new challenges and opportunities with confidence, knowing that you have the skills and mindset to succeed.

Overall, by cultivating adaptability in the workplace, you can mitigate the fear of being replaced and ensure that you remain a valuable and irreplaceable member of your organization. Embrace change, learn new skills, and demonstrate your willingness to grow - your future self will thank you for it.

Chapter 7: Thriving in a Culture of Replaceability

Leveraging Networking and Relationships

In the competitive world of business, it is essential to leverage networking and relationships to stay ahead and secure your position in the industry. Building a strong network of contacts and nurturing relationships with key stakeholders can open doors to new opportunities, help you stay informed about industry trends, and provide valuable support when faced with challenges.

Networking is not just about collecting business cards or connecting on LinkedIn; it is about building meaningful relationships based on trust, mutual respect, and a shared interest in each other's success. By investing time and effort into cultivating these relationships, you can create a network of allies who will support you in your career journey and help you navigate the ups and downs of the business world.

One key aspect of leveraging networking and relationships is the concept of reciprocity. By offering help, support, and valuable insights to your network, you can build goodwill and establish yourself as a valuable resource to others. In return, you can expect the same level of support and assistance when you need it most.

Another important aspect of leveraging networking and relationships is the power of collaboration. By working together with your network to achieve common goals, you can amplify your impact, leverage each other's strengths, and create win-win situations that benefit everyone involved.

Having a strong network of contacts and nurturing relationships with key stakeholders can be a game-changer. By leveraging networking and relationships effectively, you can position yourself for success, stay ahead of the competition, and secure your place in the industry for years to come.

Embracing Lifelong Learning and Development

In business, the only constant is change. As technology advances and industries evolve, the need for continuous learning and development becomes more crucial than ever before. For business people, entrepreneurs, managers, and the general public, understanding the value of lifelong learning is essential for personal and professional growth. In a world where everyone is replaceable, the key to staying relevant and indispensable is to continuously update your skills, knowledge, and competencies.

By embracing lifelong learning and development, individuals can adapt to new technologies, trends, and market demands. This not only enhances their own capabilities but also positions them as valuable assets within their organizations. In a world where job roles are constantly evolving, those who invest in their own learning are more likely to succeed and thrive in the long run.

Moreover, lifelong learning fosters a growth mindset, resilience, and adaptability – qualities that are essential for navigating the uncertainties of the business world. By continuously seeking new knowledge and experiences, individuals can broaden their perspectives, enhance their problem-solving abilities, and drive innovation within their organizations.

"Embracing Lifelong Learning and Development" is not just a choice, but a necessity for anyone looking to succeed in today's business environment. By committing to ongoing growth and development, individuals can future-proof their careers, unlock new opportunities, and ultimately, stand out in a world where everyone is replaceable.

Finding Purpose and Fulfillment Beyond Job Titles

Today is easy to get caught up in the idea that our worth is tied solely to our job titles. However, true fulfillment and purpose go beyond the confines of a simple label. In this section, we will explore ways to find meaning and satisfaction in our work and lives beyond the limitations of our job titles.

One key aspect to consider is the importance of aligning our values and passions with our work. When we are able to connect our personal beliefs and interests with the work we do, we can find a deeper sense of fulfillment and purpose. This may involve taking on projects that align with our values, seeking out opportunities for growth and learning, or even exploring new roles that better suit our passions.

Another important factor to consider is the impact we have on others and the world around us. By focusing on how we can make a positive difference in the lives of those around us, we can find a greater sense of purpose in our work. Whether it's through mentorship, volunteer work, or simply going the extra mile to help a colleague, the impact we have on others can be truly fulfilling.

Ultimately, finding purpose and fulfillment beyond job titles requires a shift in mindset. Instead of defining ourselves solely by our roles in the workplace, we must look inward and discover what truly drives us and brings us joy. By aligning our values, passions, and desire to make a difference, we can find true fulfillment in our work and lives, regardless of our job titles.

Chapter 8: Embracing Change and Leading with Replaceability

Leading by Example

In business, one of the most effective ways to inspire and motivate those around you is by leading by example. Whether you are a business owner, entrepreneur, manager, or employee, demonstrating the qualities and behaviors you want to see in others can have a powerful impact on the success of your team and your organization as a whole.

Leading by example means more than just talking the talk – it means walking the walk. It means showing up early, staying late, and putting in the extra effort to get the job done right. It means being honest, ethical, and transparent in all your dealings. It means treating others with respect, kindness, and empathy. It means taking risks, making tough decisions, and owning up to your mistakes.

When you lead by example, you set the tone for your team and create a culture of excellence, accountability, and integrity. Your actions speak louder than words, and your behavior will be emulated by those around you. By demonstrating a strong work ethic, a positive attitude, and a commitment to excellence, you can inspire others to do the same.

In a world where everyone is replaceable, leading by example is more important than ever. By showing your team that you are willing to roll up your sleeves and do whatever it takes to succeed, you can earn their trust, respect, and loyalty. You can build a team of dedicated, motivated individuals who will go above and beyond to help your organization thrive.

So, whether you are a seasoned business professional or just starting out in your career, remember that leadership is not about titles or positions – it's about actions and behaviors. Lead by example, and watch as your team rises to meet the challenge, exceed expectations, and achieve great things together.

Fostering a Culture of Innovation and Adaptability

Fostering a Culture of Innovation and Adaptability is key in today's business world. In order to stay ahead of the curve and remain competitive, businesses must constantly evolve and adapt to new challenges and opportunities. This subchapter explores the importance of creating a culture that embraces innovation and encourages employees to think outside the box.

Innovation is the driving force behind success in business. It allows companies to stay relevant, meet customer needs, and outperform the competition. By fostering a culture of innovation, businesses can empower their employees to come up with creative solutions to problems and explore new ideas that can lead to growth and success.

Adaptability is equally important in today's business world. With technology changing at a rapid pace and market trends evolving constantly, businesses must be able to pivot and adjust their strategies to meet new demands. By creating a culture that values adaptability, businesses can ensure that they are able to respond quickly to changes in the market and stay ahead of the curve.

This subchapter will provide practical tips and strategies for fostering a culture of innovation and adaptability within your organization. From encouraging creativity and risk-taking to promoting a growth mindset and embracing failure as a learning opportunity, there are many ways to create a workplace that thrives on innovation and adaptability.

Whether you are a business person, entrepreneur, manager, or member of the general public, the principles of fostering a culture of innovation and adaptability are applicable to all. By embracing these ideas, you can position yourself and your organization for success in an ever-changing world where everyone is replaceable.

Empowering Others to Embrace Replaceability

In business, one of the harsh realities that we must all come to terms with is the fact that everyone is replaceable. While this may sound daunting, it is also a powerful concept that can drive innovation, growth, and success within organizations. Empowering others to embrace replaceability is crucial in today's competitive landscape.

As business people, entrepreneurs, managers, and members of the general public, we must understand that no one is irreplaceable. This mindset shift can be liberating, as it allows individuals to focus on developing their skills, knowledge, and abilities to stay ahead in their careers. By embracing replaceability, we open ourselves up to new opportunities for growth and advancement.

Empowering others to embrace replaceability also fosters a culture of collaboration and teamwork within organizations. When individuals understand that their role is not set in stone, they are more likely to work together, share knowledge, and support one another in achieving common goals. This creates a more dynamic and adaptable workforce that can respond quickly to changing market conditions and emerging trends.

As leaders, it is our responsibility to instill this mindset within our teams. By encouraging a culture of continuous learning, adaptability, and innovation, we can prepare our organizations for the future and ensure their long-term success. Embracing replaceability is not about devaluing individuals, but rather empowering them to reach their full potential and contribute to the collective success of the organization.

Empowering others to embrace replaceability is essential in business. By fostering a culture of adaptability, collaboration, and continuous learning, we can position ourselves and our organizations for success in an ever-changing landscape. Embrace replaceability, and watch your team thrive.

Chapter 9: The Power of Transferable Skills

Identifying and honing transferable skills

In business, one thing is certain - everyone is replaceable. In order to stay competitive and relevant in the ever-evolving landscape of the business world, it is essential to identify and hone transferable skills that can help you stand out and thrive in any role.

Identifying transferable skills involves taking a closer look at your unique strengths, experiences, and abilities that can be applied to a variety of roles and industries. These skills can include communication, problem-solving, leadership, adaptability, and critical thinking. By recognizing and developing these skills, you can position yourself as a valuable asset to any organization, regardless of the specific job title or industry.

Honing transferable skills requires ongoing effort and dedication. This can involve seeking out opportunities for professional development, taking on new challenges, and seeking feedback from colleagues and mentors. Additionally, it is important to stay current with industry trends and developments, and continuously seek out new ways to expand your skill set.

By focusing on identifying and honing transferable skills, you can increase your value as a professional and enhance your ability to succeed in a competitive business environment. Whether you are a seasoned entrepreneur, a manager looking to advance in your career, or simply someone looking to stay ahead of the curve, developing transferable skills is key to remaining relevant and indispensable.

How Transferable Skills Enhance Employability

The concept of employability is a crucial consideration for both employees and employers. One way to enhance employability is by focusing on developing transferable skills. These skills are not specific to a particular job or industry, but can be applied across various roles and sectors.

For business people, entrepreneurs, managers, and the general public, understanding the importance of transferable skills is essential for staying competitive in the job market. In a world where everyone is replaceable, having a versatile skill set can set you apart from the crowd. Employers are increasingly looking for candidates who can bring a diverse range of skills to the table, allowing them to quickly adapt to changing business needs.

Transferable skills such as communication, problem-solving, leadership, and time management are highly sought after business skills. These skills not only make individuals more employable but also help them excel in their current roles and advance their careers. By focusing on developing these skills, individuals can future-proof their careers and remain valuable assets to their organizations.

In "Next in Line," we explore practical strategies for identifying and honing transferable skills, as well as how to effectively showcase them to potential employers. By understanding the role of transferable skills in enhancing employability, individuals can position themselves for success in an increasingly competitive job market. Whether you are a seasoned professional or just starting out in your career, investing in transferable skills is a smart move that can pay dividends in the long run.

Transitioning between industries with transferable skills

Transitioning between industries can be a daunting task, especially if you feel like your skills are only applicable to your current field. However, it's important to remember that many skills are transferable across industries, and with a little creativity and determination, you can successfully make the shift.

One of the keys to transitioning between industries is identifying your transferable skills. These are the skills that you have developed throughout your career that can be applied to a variety of roles and industries. For example, if you have strong communication skills, project management experience, or leadership abilities, these are all skills that are highly sought after in almost any industry.

Once you have identified your transferable skills, it's important to tailor your resume and cover letter to highlight these skills and demonstrate how they are relevant to the new industry you are targeting. This can help you stand out to potential employers and show them that you have what it takes to succeed in a new role.

Networking is also key when transitioning between industries. Reach out to contacts in the industry you are interested in, attend industry events and conferences, and join professional organizations to expand your network and learn more about the new field you are entering. Building relationships with people who are already established in the industry can open doors and help you navigate the transition more smoothly.

Overall, transitioning between industries with transferable skills is definitely possible with the right mindset and approach. By identifying your transferable skills, tailoring your materials, and networking effectively, you can successfully make the leap to a new industry and thrive in your new role.

Chapter 10: Embracing Change

Overcoming Resistance to Change

Resistance to change is a common challenge in the business world. Whether it's a new technology implementation, a shift in company culture, or a reorganization of teams, people tend to resist change because it disrupts their comfort zone and challenges their established routines. However, in order to thrive, it is crucial for individuals and organizations to embrace change and adapt quickly.

One key strategy for overcoming resistance to change is effective communication. It is essential for leaders to communicate the reasons behind the change, the benefits it will bring, and the potential challenges that may arise. By being transparent and open with employees, managers can help build trust and create a sense of shared purpose, which can motivate people to accept and even embrace the change.

Another important aspect of overcoming resistance to change is involving employees in the decision-making process. When people feel like their opinions are valued and that they have a say in how the change will be implemented, they are more likely to be supportive and engaged. This can also help identify potential obstacles and develop solutions that address the concerns of those who are resistant to the change.

In addition, providing training and support to employees during the transition period can help alleviate anxieties and build confidence. By investing in professional development and offering resources to help people navigate the change, organizations can empower their employees to adapt and thrive in the new environment.

Overall, overcoming resistance to change requires a combination of effective communication, employee involvement, and support. By recognizing the importance of change and having a proactive approach to managing it, businesses can successfully navigate through periods of transition and emerge stronger and more resilient than before.

Techniques for Embracing Change in the Workplace

Change is inevitable, whether it's due to advancements in technology, shifts in market trends, or organizational restructuring, the ability to adapt to change is crucial for success in the workplace. In this subchapter, we will explore techniques for embracing change in the workplace, helping you navigate the ever-evolving landscape of business with confidence and grace.

One technique for embracing change is to cultivate a growth mindset. This involves viewing change as an opportunity for learning and personal development, rather than a threat to your stability or comfort. By approaching change with a positive and open mindset, you can more easily adapt to new challenges and opportunities that come your way.

Another technique is to practice resilience in the face of change. Resilience involves the ability to bounce back from setbacks and challenges, and to persevere in the face of adversity. By building your resilience muscle, you can weather the storms of change with grace and determination, emerging stronger and more capable on the other side.

Additionally, it's important to communicate openly and honestly with colleagues and superiors during times of change. By fostering a culture of transparency and open communication, you can create a sense of trust and collaboration that will help you navigate change more effectively as a team.

Ultimately, embracing change in the workplace requires a combination of mindset, skillset, and communication. By cultivating a growth mindset, practicing resilience, and fostering open communication, you can navigate the world of replaceability in business with confidence and adaptability. Remember, change is inevitable – it's how you respond to it that counts.

How to Successfully Implement Organizational Change

Implementing organizational change can be a daunting task, but it is essential for businesses to adapt and stay competitive. Successful implementation of organizational change requires careful planning, effective communication, and strong leadership. In this subchapter, we will discuss some key strategies for successfully implementing organizational change.

First and foremost, it is important to clearly define the reasons for change and communicate them to all stakeholders. Whether the change is driven by market forces, technological advancements, or internal factors, everyone in the organization should understand why change is necessary and how it will benefit the company in the long run.

Next, it is crucial to involve employees in the change process. Employees are more likely to support and embrace change if they feel that their input is valued and that they have a say in the decision-making process. This can be achieved through regular communication, feedback sessions, and involving employees in planning and implementing the change.

Strong leadership is also key to successfully implementing organizational change. Leaders should be visible, accessible, and supportive throughout the change process. They should clearly communicate the vision for change, provide direction and guidance, and inspire and motivate employees to embrace the change.

Finally, it is important to monitor and evaluate the progress of the change initiative. Regularly assess whether the desired outcomes are being achieved, and make adjustments as needed. Celebrate small wins along the way to keep employees motivated and engaged.

Successfully implementing organizational change requires careful planning, effective communication, strong leadership, and employee involvement. By following these strategies, businesses can navigate the challenges of change and emerge stronger and more competitive in the ever-evolving business world.

Chapter 11: The Downside of Dependency

Pitfalls of relying too heavily on key individuals

In the world of business, it is common for key individuals to emerge as leaders within their organizations. These individuals often possess unique skills, knowledge, and experience that make them invaluable assets to their companies. However, relying too heavily on these key individuals can lead to a number of pitfalls that can ultimately harm the organization.

One of the biggest pitfalls of relying too heavily on key individuals is the risk of burnout. When a single individual is shouldering a heavy workload or is responsible for critical tasks, they can quickly become overwhelmed and stressed. This can lead to decreased productivity, increased absenteeism, and even long-term health issues. Additionally, if a key individual were to leave the organization suddenly, it could leave a significant gap that is difficult to fill, leading to disruptions in operations and potential financial losses.

Another pitfall of relying too heavily on key individuals is the risk of stagnation. When one person is seen as the sole source of knowledge or expertise within an organization, it can stifle innovation and creativity. Other team members may feel discouraged from sharing their ideas or taking on new challenges, leading to a lack of growth and development within the organization.

To avoid these pitfalls, it is important for business leaders to create a culture of collaboration and teamwork within their organizations. By encouraging knowledge sharing, cross-training, and mentorship programs, companies can ensure that no one individual holds all the keys to success. This not only reduces the risk of burnout and stagnation but also helps to build a more resilient and adaptable workforce.

While key individuals can play a valuable role within an organization, it is important not to rely too heavily on any one person. By fostering a culture of teamwork and collaboration, businesses can mitigate the risks associated with individual replaceability and ensure long-term success. Remember, everyone is replaceable, and it is essential to plan for the future by building a strong and diverse team.

Risk management strategies for reducing dependency

In the competitive landscape of business, the risk of becoming too dependent on key individuals or resources can be a major threat to the sustainability of any organization. To mitigate this risk and ensure long-term success, it is essential for businesses to adopt effective risk management strategies that focus on reducing dependency.

One of the key strategies for reducing dependency is to diversify your talent pool. By hiring and developing a team of skilled individuals with diverse backgrounds and expertise, businesses can minimize the risk of being heavily reliant on a single individual. This not only increases the resilience of the organization but also fosters a culture of collaboration and innovation.

Another important risk management strategy is to cross-train employees. By providing opportunities for employees to learn new skills and take on different responsibilities, businesses can ensure that there are multiple individuals capable of performing critical tasks. This not only reduces dependency on specific individuals but also increases the overall efficiency and effectiveness of the organization.

Furthermore, businesses should invest in technology and automation to reduce dependency on manual processes and streamline operations. By leveraging technology to automate repetitive tasks and streamline workflows, businesses can reduce the risk of human error and enhance productivity.

Ultimately, the key to reducing dependency lies in proactive risk management and strategic planning. By implementing these risk management strategies, businesses can strengthen their resilience, adaptability, and long-term viability in an ever-changing business environment. Remember, in the world of business, everyone is replaceable, and it is essential to prepare for the unexpected.

Balancing delegation with accountability

In the world of business, one of the most crucial skills for leaders to master is the delicate balance between delegation and accountability. Delegation is essential for a successful organization, as it allows leaders to distribute tasks and responsibilities among their team members, freeing up time and resources to focus on higher-level strategic initiatives. However, without proper accountability measures in place, delegation can quickly lead to chaos and confusion.

To effectively balance delegation with accountability, leaders must establish clear expectations and guidelines for their team members. This includes defining roles and responsibilities, setting goals and deadlines, and providing the necessary resources and support for employees to succeed in their tasks. By clearly communicating expectations upfront, leaders can ensure that everyone is on the same page and working towards a common goal.

Accountability is equally important in the delegation process. Leaders must hold their team members responsible for their actions and outcomes, providing feedback and guidance as needed to ensure that tasks are completed effectively and efficiently. This helps to foster a culture of ownership and responsibility within the organization, where team members feel empowered to take initiative and deliver results.

By striking the right balance between delegation and accountability, leaders can create a dynamic and high-performing team that is capable of achieving great things. When everyone understands their roles and responsibilities, and is held accountable for their actions, the entire organization can work together towards success. Remember, in the world of business, everyone is replaceable, but by mastering the art of balancing delegation with accountability, leaders can ensure that their team is irreplaceable.

Chapter 12: The Myth of the Irreplaceable Leader

Examining the Cult of Personality in Leadership

In the competitive world of business, leaders often find themselves in the spotlight, hailed as visionary and charismatic figures who can inspire their teams to achieve greatness. However, this cult of personality surrounding leaders can sometimes lead to detrimental effects on the organization as a whole.

Examining the cult of personality in leadership is crucial for understanding the dynamics at play within a company. When a leader becomes too focused on their own personal brand and image, they may lose sight of the bigger picture and the needs of their team. This can result in a toxic work environment where employees feel undervalued and unappreciated.

Moreover, when a leader is placed on a pedestal and treated as irreplaceable, it can create a power imbalance within the organization. This not only stifles innovation and creativity but also hinders the development of future leaders within the company. By examining the cult of personality in leadership, we can begin to break down these barriers and foster a more collaborative and inclusive work environment.

In "Next in Line: Navigating the World of Replaceability in Business," we explore the importance of humility and self-awareness in leadership. We challenge the notion that leaders are infallible and encourage a more transparent and open approach to leadership. By recognizing that everyone is replaceable, we can create a culture that values teamwork and collective success over individual glory.

Business people, entrepreneurs, managers, and the general public can all benefit from examining the cult of personality in leadership. By understanding the impact that leaders have on their organizations, we can work towards building stronger, more resilient businesses that thrive on collaboration and inclusivity.

Consequences of Leader-Centric Organizations

In the business world, many organizations operate under a leader-centric model, where one individual holds the majority of power and influence. While this may seem efficient and effective in the short term, there are several consequences that can arise from this approach.

One major consequence of leader-centric organizations is the risk of decision-making becoming centralized in the hands of a single individual. This can lead to a lack of diversity in perspectives and ideas, as well as a higher likelihood of decisions being influenced by personal biases or agendas. In addition, if the leader were to suddenly leave the organization, there may be a significant power vacuum that could disrupt operations and cause chaos.

Another consequence of leader-centric organizations is the potential for employee disengagement and lack of motivation. When employees feel like their contributions are not valued or that their opinions are not taken into consideration, morale can quickly decline. This can result in decreased productivity, increased turnover rates, and a negative company culture overall.

Furthermore, leader-centric organizations can hinder innovation and creativity. When all decisions are made by one person, there is limited room for experimentation and risk-taking. This can stifle growth and prevent the organization from adapting to changing market conditions or technological advancements.

Overall, while leader-centric organizations may offer some short-term benefits in terms of efficiency and decisiveness, the long-term consequences can be detrimental to the success and sustainability of the business. It is important for business people, entrepreneurs, managers, and the general public to recognize the risks associated with this model and consider alternative approaches that prioritize collaboration, empowerment, and inclusivity. Remember, everyone is replaceable, including the leader.

Cultivating Leadership Pipelines

In the aggressive world of business, cultivating leadership pipelines is crucial for ensuring the long-term success and sustainability of any organization. Understanding the significance of cultivating leadership pipelines is essential for ensuring smooth transitions and continuity in leadership roles. By actively identifying and developing potential leaders within the organization, companies can mitigate the risks associated with key personnel changes and ensure a steady supply of talent to fill critical roles.

One of the key principles highlighted in this book is the idea that everyone is replaceable. While this may sound harsh, it serves as a reminder that no individual is indispensable in an organization. By acknowledging this reality and actively working to cultivate a pipeline of future leaders, companies can avoid disruptions and maintain business continuity in the face of unexpected departures or retirements.

Through effective leadership development programs, mentorship opportunities, and succession planning strategies, organizations can proactively groom their next generation of leaders. By investing in the growth and development of their employees, companies can create a culture of continuous learning and professional advancement that benefits both the individual and the organization as a whole.

Cultivating leadership pipelines is a critical aspect of navigating the world of replaceability in business. By recognizing the importance of developing future leaders and taking proactive steps to nurture talent within the organization, companies can position themselves for long-term success and sustainability in an ever-changing business environment.

Chapter 13: Creating Redundancy for Resilience

Importance of Redundancy in Business Operations

In the world of business, the concept of redundancy often carries a negative connotation. Many see it as unnecessary duplication or waste of resources. However, in the ever-changing landscape of business operations, redundancy plays a crucial role in ensuring continuity and stability.

The importance of redundancy in business operations cannot be understated. It serves as a safety net, providing backup systems and processes in case of unexpected failures or disruptions. As a result, businesses cannot afford to have a single point of failure. Redundancy helps mitigate risks and minimizes the impact of potential disruptions on the overall operations.

For business people, entrepreneurs, managers, and the general public, understanding the value of redundancy is essential for long-term success. By incorporating redundancy into their operations, businesses can increase resilience and adaptability, allowing them to navigate through unforeseen challenges with ease.

In this book, readers will learn how to strategically implement redundancy in their operations to enhance efficiency and minimize downtime. By embracing redundancy, businesses can ensure continuity of services, maintain customer satisfaction, and protect their reputation in the market.

In a world where everyone is replaceable, the ability to adapt and thrive in the face of uncertainty is key. Redundancy provides businesses with the flexibility and security they need to stay ahead of the curve and remain competitive in the ever-evolving business landscape. Embracing redundancy is not just a choice, but a necessity for survival in today's volatile business environment.

Designing Systems with Redundancy in Mind

It is crucial to design systems with redundancy in mind. This means building systems that can withstand failures and disruptions without causing a major impact on the overall operations of the business. As a result, understanding the concept of redundancy is essential for ensuring the continuity and success of your operations. By designing systems with redundancy in mind, you are essentially creating a safety net that can prevent catastrophic failures and minimize the impact of unexpected events.

Redundancy can take various forms, such as backup systems, duplicate processes, or cross-trained employees. By having these redundancies in place, you can ensure that your business can continue to function even in the face of challenges.

In the niche of "Everyone is Replaceable," designing systems with redundancy in mind is even more critical. This mindset acknowledges that no individual is indispensable and that every role within a business should have backups and fail-safes in place. By implementing redundancy in your systems, you are not only protecting your business from disruptions but also empowering your team to handle any situation that may arise.

So, whether you are a seasoned entrepreneur or a newcomer to the business world, it is essential to consider the importance of redundancy in your systems. By doing so, you can position your business for long-term success and resilience in the face of uncertainty.

Lessons from Failures Due to Lack of Redundancy

In the world of business, one of the most important lessons that can be learned is the necessity of having redundancy in place. When a company fails to implement redundancy measures, it can lead to disastrous consequences that could have easily been avoided. In this subchapter, we will explore some key lessons that can be gleaned from failures due to lack of redundancy.

One of the most glaring lessons is the importance of having backup systems in place. Whether it's backup power sources, data storage systems, or personnel, having redundancy ensures that the business can continue to operate smoothly even in the face of unexpected challenges. Without these backup measures, a single point of failure can bring the entire operation to a grinding halt.

Another important lesson is the need for diversity in skills and knowledge among employees. When a company relies too heavily on a single individual or a small group of people, it leaves itself vulnerable to disruptions if those individuals are unavailable for any reason. By cross-training employees and ensuring that multiple people are capable of handling key tasks, a business can mitigate the risks associated with relying too heavily on any one person.

Lastly, failures due to lack of redundancy highlight the importance of regularly reviewing and updating contingency plans. As circumstances change and new risks emerge, it's crucial for businesses to adapt their redundancy measures accordingly. A failure to do so can leave a company ill-prepared to handle unexpected challenges when they arise.

The failures that result from lack of redundancy serve as valuable lessons for all businesses. By implementing backup systems, fostering diversity among employees, and regularly updating contingency plans, companies can better position themselves to weather any storm that comes their way.

Chapter 14: The Future of Business and Replaceability

Trends Shaping the Future of Work

It is crucial for business people, entrepreneurs, managers, and the general public to stay informed about the trends shaping the future of work. With the rise of technology, globalization, and changing consumer preferences, the way we work is constantly evolving. In this book, we will explore the key trends that are shaping the future of work and how individuals can adapt to stay ahead in their careers.

One of the most significant trends shaping the future of work is the increasing use of automation and artificial intelligence. As technology continues to advance, many routine tasks and jobs are being automated, leading to a shift in the skills required in the workforce. Business people and entrepreneurs need to stay updated on the latest technological developments and adapt their skills to remain relevant in the job market.

Another trend that is shaping the future of work is the rise of the gig economy. With more people choosing to work as freelancers or independent contractors, traditional employment models are being disrupted. Managers and business people need to be aware of this trend and consider how they can leverage the gig economy to their advantage.

Additionally, the growing emphasis on diversity and inclusion in the workplace is another important trend that is shaping the future of work. Business people and managers need to create inclusive work environments that celebrate diversity and empower employees from all backgrounds to succeed.

By staying informed about these trends and adapting to the changing landscape of work, individuals can position themselves for success in the future. "Next in Line: Navigating the World of Replaceability in Business" provides valuable insights and strategies for navigating these trends and thriving in the evolving world of work.

Embracing Technological Advancements

Technological advancements are constantly reshaping the way we do business. As the digital landscape continues to evolve, it is crucial for business people, entrepreneurs, managers, and the general public to embrace these changes in order to stay competitive and relevant in their respective industries.

One of the key benefits of embracing technological advancements is the increased efficiency and productivity that they bring to businesses. Automation, artificial intelligence, and other cutting-edge technologies can streamline processes, reduce human error, and free up valuable time and resources for more strategic tasks. By leveraging these tools, businesses can improve their bottom line and gain a competitive edge in the marketplace.

In addition, embracing technological advancements can also open up new opportunities for innovation and growth. By staying abreast of the latest trends and developments in technology, businesses can identify new ways to serve their customers, expand into new markets, and differentiate themselves from their competitors. This mindset of continuous learning and adaptation is essential for staying ahead in an increasingly dynamic and unpredictable business environment.

However, it is important to recognize that with these advancements comes the risk of being replaced. In the age of digital disruption, no one is immune to the threat of obsolescence. This is why it is crucial for business people, entrepreneurs, managers, and the general public to continuously upskill, reskill, and adapt to the changing technological landscape in order to remain valuable and irreplaceable in their roles.

By embracing technological advancements and taking proactive steps to stay ahead of the curve, individuals and businesses can position themselves for long-term success and relevance in an ever-evolving world. The key is to approach change with an open mind, a willingness to learn, and a commitment to continuous improvement.

Creating a Sustainable and Resilient Business Model

Creating a sustainable and resilient business model is essential in business. In order to thrive and stay competitive, businesses must adapt and evolve to meet the needs of their customers and the demands of the market. This subchapter will explore key strategies and principles for creating a business model that is not only sustainable but also resilient in the face of challenges and disruptions.

One of the first steps in creating a sustainable and resilient business model is to focus on innovation and creativity. Businesses that are able to think outside the box and come up with new ideas and solutions are more likely to succeed in the long run. This may involve investing in research and development, fostering a culture of creativity within the organization, and constantly seeking out new opportunities for growth and expansion.

Another important aspect of creating a sustainable and resilient business model is to build strong relationships with customers, suppliers, and other stakeholders. By creating a network of trusted partners and collaborators, businesses can ensure that they have the support and resources they need to weather any storms that may come their way. This may involve developing strong communication channels, negotiating fair and mutually beneficial agreements, and always putting the needs of their partners first.

In addition, businesses must also focus on sustainability and social responsibility in order to create a business model that is not only profitable but also ethical and environmentally friendly. By embracing sustainable practices, businesses can reduce their impact on the planet, attract socially conscious customers, and build a positive reputation in the marketplace.

Overall, creating a sustainable and resilient business model requires a combination of innovation, collaboration, and social responsibility. By following these principles and strategies, businesses can position themselves for long-term success and ensure that they are able to adapt and thrive in an ever-changing world.

Chapter 15: Navigating Layoffs and Restructuring

Ethical Considerations in Workforce Reduction

In the world of business, workforce reduction is often seen as a necessary evil in order to improve efficiency and cut costs. However, it is important to consider the ethical implications of such actions. In this subchapter, we will explore the ethical considerations that should be taken into account when making decisions about reducing the workforce.

One of the key ethical considerations in workforce reduction is the impact it will have on the employees who are being let go. It is important to treat these individuals with respect and dignity, and to provide them with support and resources to help them transition to a new job or career. This may include offering career counseling, resume writing assistance, or even financial assistance to help them through this difficult time.

Another ethical consideration is the impact that workforce reduction will have on the remaining employees. It is important to communicate openly and honestly with employees about the reasons for the reduction, and to provide them with reassurance and support during this uncertain time. It is also important to ensure that the workload of the remaining employees is manageable and that they are not being overburdened as a result of the reduction.

Finally, it is important to consider the impact that workforce reduction will have on the community and society as a whole. When large numbers of people are laid off from their jobs, this can have a ripple effect on the local economy and social fabric. It is important for businesses to take this into account and to consider ways to minimize the negative impact on the community.

While workforce reduction may be a necessary business decision, it is important to approach it with careful consideration of the ethical implications. By treating employees with respect and dignity, providing support for those who are let go, and considering the impact on the remaining employees and the community, businesses can navigate the difficult process of workforce reduction in a more ethical and responsible manner.

Supporting Employees Through Transitions

In business, transitions are inevitable. Whether it's a reorganization, a merger, or simply a change in leadership, employees are often left feeling uncertain about their future within the company. As a business leader, it is crucial to support your employees through these transitions to ensure morale and productivity remain high.

One of the most important ways to support employees during times of change is through open and honest communication. Keep your team informed about what is happening within the company and how it may impact them personally. Address any concerns or questions they may have, and be transparent about the reasons behind the changes taking place.

It's also essential to provide your employees with the resources they need to navigate these transitions successfully. This could include additional training or professional development opportunities to help them adapt to new roles or responsibilities. Offering emotional support through counseling services or employee assistance programs can also be beneficial during times of uncertainty.

Another way to support employees through transitions is by fostering a sense of community and teamwork within the organization. Encourage collaboration and communication among team members, and provide opportunities for them to connect outside of work. Building strong relationships among employees can help them feel more supported and valued during times of change.

Ultimately, supporting employees through transitions is not only beneficial for their well-being but also for the overall success of the business. By showing empathy, providing resources, and fostering a sense of community, you can help your team navigate change with confidence and resilience. Remember, everyone is replaceable, but taking care of your employees will help ensure they choose to stay.

Rebuilding Morale After Layoffs

Regrettably, layoffs are unfortunately a common occurrence. Whether due to financial constraints, restructuring, or other reasons, the reality is sooner or later most of us will face the threat of layoffs. However, what sets successful companies apart is how they handle the aftermath of layoffs and work towards rebuilding morale within the organization.

After a round of layoffs, it is crucial for business leaders to address the emotional impact on both the employees who were let go and those who remain. Transparency and open communication are key in rebuilding trust and morale. Employees need to understand why the layoffs were necessary and what steps the company is taking to move forward. This will help alleviate fears and uncertainty among the remaining staff.

It is also important for leaders to show empathy and support to those who were laid off. Providing resources for job hunting, resume building, and emotional support can go a long way in helping them transition to their next opportunity. This gesture of goodwill can also help boost morale among the remaining employees, showing that the company cares about its people.

In order to rebuild morale, it is essential for leaders to focus on the future and rally the team around a common goal. Setting clear objectives, providing opportunities for growth and development, and recognizing employees for their hard work can help re-energize the organization. By fostering a positive and supportive work environment, leaders can inspire loyalty and dedication among their team members.

Remember, in the world of business, everyone is replaceable. But by handling layoffs with empathy, transparency, and a focus on rebuilding morale, companies can emerge stronger and more resilient than ever before.

Chapter 16: Strategies for Personal Branding

Leveraging Personal Branding for Career Resilience

The concept of career resilience has never been more important. With the rise of automation, artificial intelligence, and other disruptive technologies, the notion that "everyone is replaceable" has become a harsh reality for many workers. However, there are ways to ensure that you remain valuable and indispensable in the eyes of employers, clients, and colleagues.

One powerful tool for building career resilience is leveraging personal branding. Personal branding is the practice of managing and promoting your unique skills, strengths, and values to create a strong and memorable professional identity. By developing a strong personal brand, you can differentiate yourself from the competition, showcase your expertise, and build a reputation as a trusted and reliable professional.

One of the key benefits of personal branding is that it allows you to control how you are perceived by others. By carefully crafting your online presence, including your social media profiles, website, and professional networking platforms, you can shape the way that others see you and position yourself as an expert in your field. This can help you stand out in a crowded job market, attract new clients or customers, and open up new opportunities for career advancement.

Furthermore, a strong personal brand can help you weather the storms of job insecurity and economic uncertainty. By demonstrating your value and expertise consistently and authentically, you can build a loyal following of supporters and advocates who will vouch for your skills and recommend you to others. This network of supporters can provide valuable connections, referrals, and opportunities that can help you bounce back quickly from setbacks and continue to thrive in your career.

Personal branding is a powerful tool for building career resilience in business. By investing time and effort into developing and promoting your unique professional identity, you can position yourself as a valuable and irreplaceable asset in any organization or industry. So, take control of your personal brand and make sure that you are next in line for success.

Making yourself Unforgettable

It's easy to feel like just another cog in the machine. With the constant threat of being replaced looming over our heads, how can we set ourselves apart and make ourselves unforgettable in the eyes of our colleagues, bosses, and clients?

The key to making yourself unforgettable lies in your ability to consistently deliver exceptional work. This means going above and beyond what is expected of you, taking on new challenges, and constantly striving for improvement. By demonstrating your value through your actions and results, you can prove that you are an indispensable asset to your team.

Building strong relationships is another crucial aspect of making yourself unforgettable. Take the time to get to know your colleagues on a personal level, show genuine interest in their lives and work, and be a supportive and reliable team player. By fostering strong connections with those around you, you can create a positive and memorable impression that will set you apart from the rest.

Additionally, it's important to actively seek out opportunities for growth and development. Stay up-to-date on industry trends, attend workshops and seminars, and continuously expand your skill set. By demonstrating a commitment to your own personal and professional growth, you show that you are a valuable and irreplaceable asset to any organization.

Ultimately, making yourself unforgettable requires a combination of hard work, dedication, and a positive attitude. By consistently delivering exceptional results, building strong relationships, and seeking out opportunities for growth, you can set yourself apart from the competition and prove that you are truly irreplaceable in the world of business.

Building a Strong Employee-Employer Relation

Building a strong employee-employer relationship is crucial in any business setting, regardless of whether you believe in the mantra that "everyone is replaceable." While it is true that individuals can be replaced, fostering a positive and respectful work environment can lead to increased employee satisfaction, productivity, and ultimately, retention.

One of the key components of building a strong employee-employer relationship is effective communication. Employers should strive to maintain open lines of communication with their employees, providing regular feedback, listening to their concerns, and ensuring that they feel heard and valued. This not only helps to build trust and mutual respect but also allows for issues to be addressed and resolved before they escalate.

Creating a culture of transparency and fairness is also essential in developing a strong relationship between employees and employers. Employees should feel confident that they are being treated equitably and that decisions are being made in a transparent manner. This can help to foster a sense of loyalty and commitment among employees, leading to improved morale and overall job satisfaction.

Additionally, providing opportunities for professional development and growth can help to strengthen the employee-employer relationship. Investing in your employees' skills and knowledge demonstrates that you value their contributions and are committed to their long-term success. This can lead to increased motivation and engagement, as employees feel empowered to take on new challenges and responsibilities.

While it is important to recognize that everyone is replaceable in business, it is equally important to prioritize building strong employee-employer relationships. By focusing on effective communication, transparency, fairness, and professional development, businesses can create a positive work environment that benefits both employees and employers alike.

Navigating Career Transitions with a Well-Established Personal Brand

Career transitions are inevitable. Whether you are looking to move up the corporate ladder, switch industries, or start your own business, having a well-established personal brand can make all the difference in successfully navigating these changes.

For business people, entrepreneurs, managers, and the general public, understanding the importance of a personal brand is crucial. Your personal brand is what sets you apart from the competition and showcases your unique skills, experiences, and values. It is what makes you memorable and influential in your industry.

When it comes to career transitions, having a strong personal brand can open doors and create opportunities that may not have otherwise been available to you. A well-established personal brand can help you stand out in a crowded job market, attract potential clients or investors, and build a network of valuable connections.

To effectively navigate career transitions with a well-established personal brand, it is important to first identify your unique strengths, values, and goals. What sets you apart from others in your field? What do you want to achieve in your career? By understanding these key elements, you can begin to craft a personal brand that reflects who you are and where you want to go.

Once you have established your personal brand, it is important to consistently communicate and reinforce it through your actions, interactions, and online presence. This may include updating your resume and LinkedIn profile, attending industry events, and sharing your expertise through blogs or social media.

By leveraging your well-established personal brand, you can confidently navigate career transitions and seize new opportunities with ease. Remember, in a world where everyone is replaceable, your personal brand is what makes you irreplaceable.

Chapter 17: Networking for Career Sustainability

Importance of Networking in Career Advancement

In business, networking plays a crucial role in career advancement. Whether you are a business person, entrepreneur, manager, or employee the importance of networking cannot be overstated. Networking allows you to connect with like-minded individuals, potential mentors, and industry leaders who can provide valuable insights and opportunities. By expanding your network, you increase your chances of being exposed to new ideas, trends, and career paths that you may not have considered otherwise. Staying ahead of the curve is essential, and networking can give you the edge you need to succeed.

For those in the niche of "Everyone is Replaceable," networking becomes even more critical. In a world where competition is fierce and job security is not guaranteed, having a strong network can be your lifeline. It can open doors to new job opportunities, partnerships, and collaborations that can help you stay relevant and indispensable in your field.

Furthermore, networking is not just about what you can gain from others but also about what you can offer. By being a valuable and supportive member of your network, you can build trust and credibility, which can lead to mutually beneficial relationships that can advance your career in ways you never imagined.

The importance of networking in career advancement cannot be ignored. It is a powerful tool that can help you reach new heights in your professional journey, no matter what stage of your career you are in. So, start building those connections, attending industry events, and engaging with others in your field – you never know where your next opportunity may come from.

Building and Maintaining Professional Networks

Building and maintaining professional networks is crucial in today's competitive business world. In a world where everyone is replaceable, having a strong professional network can set you apart from the competition. Networking allows you to connect with like-minded individuals, potential clients, and industry experts who can help you advance in your career or grow your business. By building relationships with others in your field, you can gain valuable insights, advice, and opportunities that can benefit you in the long run.

But building a professional network is not enough; you must also maintain it. This means staying in touch with your contacts, attending networking events, and continuously expanding your circle of connections. By nurturing your relationships with others, you can ensure that your network remains strong and continues to provide you with support and opportunities.

In this subchapter, readers will learn valuable tips and strategies for building and maintaining professional networks, including the importance of authenticity, reciprocity, and consistency in networking efforts. They will also discover how to leverage social media and online platforms to expand their network and connect with professionals from around the world.

By mastering the art of networking, business people, entrepreneurs, managers, and the general public can position themselves as valuable assets in their respective industries and increase their chances of success in an increasingly competitive business landscape.

Utilizing Networks During Times of Transition

In times of transition, whether it be due to changes in leadership, restructuring within a company, or shifts in the market, one of the most valuable resources you can tap into is your network. Utilizing your network effectively can help you navigate these changes with ease and come out on top in the ever-evolving business world.

For business people, entrepreneurs, managers, and the general public, understanding the power of networking during times of transition is crucial. Your network can provide you with valuable insights, advice, and support as you navigate the uncertainties that come with change. By leveraging your connections, you can access new opportunities, stay ahead of the curve, and position yourself for success in the face of uncertainty.

Networking is not just about making connections, it's about nurturing and maintaining those connections over time. It's about building relationships based on trust, mutual respect, and a genuine desire to help one another succeed. When times get tough, your network can be a source of strength and stability, providing you with the guidance and support you need to weather the storm.

In the world of "Everyone is Replaceable," your network can set you apart from the rest. By cultivating strong relationships with colleagues, mentors, industry peers, and other professionals, you can position yourself as a valuable asset within your organization and beyond. Your network can open doors, create opportunities, and help you adapt and thrive in an ever-changing business landscape.

So, whether you're facing a major transition in your career or business, remember to leverage your network. Reach out to those in your circle for guidance, support, and collaboration. Your network is a powerful tool that can help you navigate the uncertainties of change and emerge stronger and more resilient on the other side.

Chapter 18: Conclusion

Recap of Key Takeaways

In this subchapter, we will recap some of the key takeaways from "Next in Line: Navigating the World of Replaceability in Business" that are important for business people, entrepreneurs, managers, and the general public to keep in mind.

One of the main themes of the book is the idea that everyone is replaceable in the business world. This may sound harsh, but it is a reality that we all need to accept. No matter how talented or skilled we may be, there is always someone else out there who can do our job just as well, if not better. Understanding this concept can help us stay humble and motivated to continually improve ourselves.

Another key takeaway is the importance of adaptability in today's business environment. The only way to stay ahead in the game is to be willing to learn new skills, embrace change, and think outside the box. Those who are resistant to change will quickly find themselves left behind.

Additionally, the book emphasizes the importance of building strong relationships and networking within the business world. These connections can open up new opportunities, provide valuable insights, and help us navigate the often complex and competitive landscape of business.

Lastly, "Next in Line" stresses the importance of self-awareness and continuous self-improvement. By constantly evaluating our strengths and weaknesses, setting goals, and seeking feedback from others, we can ensure that we are always growing and evolving in our careers.

Overall, the key takeaways from this book are essential reminders for anyone looking to succeed in the world of business. By embracing the idea that everyone is replaceable, staying adaptable, building strong relationships, and focusing on self-improvement, we can position ourselves for long-term success in the ever-changing business world.

Final Thoughts on Embracing Replaceability in Business

Many people fear being replaced, believing that it signifies a lack of value or worth. However, in "Next in Line: Navigating the World of Replaceability in Business," we have explored the idea that embracing replaceability can actually be a positive and empowering mindset.

Final thoughts on embracing replaceability in business are centered around the idea that by accepting and even embracing the fact that everyone is replaceable, individuals and organizations can foster a culture of innovation, adaptability, and growth. Instead of viewing replaceability as a threat, it can be seen as an opportunity for improvement and advancement.

For business people, entrepreneurs, managers, and the general public, understanding and accepting replaceability can lead to greater resilience and success in the ever-changing landscape of the business world. By recognizing that no one is indispensable, individuals can focus on developing their skills, knowledge, and abilities to stay competitive and relevant in their fields.

Moreover, embracing replaceability can also foster a sense of humility and collaboration within organizations. When individuals are open to the idea that they are replaceable, they are more likely to seek feedback, learn from others, and work together towards common goals.

The concept of replaceability should not be feared, but rather embraced as a catalyst for growth and improvement. By adopting a mindset that everyone is replaceable, individuals and organizations can position themselves for long-term success and sustainability in the dynamic world of business.

Looking Ahead: Navigating the Ever-Changing Landscape of Business

In business, one thing is certain: change is inevitable. As technology advances, markets shift, and consumer preferences evolve, businesses must constantly adapt in order to stay relevant and competitive. In this ever-changing landscape, it is crucial for business people, entrepreneurs, managers, and the general public to stay ahead of the curve and anticipate what lies ahead.

One of the key lessons to be learned from the concept of "everyone is replaceable" is the importance of staying agile and flexible in the face of change. The ability to quickly pivot and adjust to new circumstances can mean the difference between success and failure in today's business world. By keeping an eye on emerging trends, technologies, and market shifts, individuals can position themselves to take advantage of new opportunities and stay one step ahead of the competition.

Another important aspect of navigating the ever-changing landscape of business is the need for continuous learning and development. As new technologies and ways of doing business emerge, individuals must be willing to adapt and acquire new skills in order to remain relevant. This may involve pursuing additional education, attending industry conferences, or seeking out mentorship opportunities. By investing in their own growth and development, individuals can ensure that they remain valuable and irreplaceable in their respective fields.

Ultimately, the key to navigating the ever-changing landscape of business is to embrace change rather than resist it. By remaining open-minded, adaptable, and forward-thinking, individuals can position themselves for success in an increasingly dynamic and competitive business environment. So, keep looking ahead, stay informed, and be prepared to navigate the twists and turns that lie ahead in the world of business.

Don't miss out!

Visit the website below and you can sign up to receive emails whenever Dr. Jose A. Mendez publishes a new book. There's no charge and no obligation.

https://books2read.com/r/B-A-UGHEB-YYKYC

BOOKS 2 READ

Connecting independent readers to independent writers.

Did you love *Next in Line: Navigating the World of Replaceability in Business*? Then you should read *Warrior Mindset: A Veteran's Guide to Entrepreneurship and Business*[1] by Dr. Jose A. Mendez!

[2]

The journey to success for the veteran entrepreneur is a testament to the indomitable spirit and resilience of our military personnel. By embracing the warrior mindset, leveraging military experience, and building a strong support network, veterans can overcome the obstacles they encounter and achieve their entrepreneurial goals.

This book by Dr. Jose A. Mendez, an Air Force veteran, serves as a tribute, a guide, and a source of inspiration for veterans, business people, and military personnel alike. It is his hope that through the lessons and insights shared within these pages, we can empower and support those embarking on the warrior entrepreneur's journey to success. Remember,

---

1. https://books2read.com/u/bp12Mg

2. https://books2read.com/u/bp12Mg

the warrior within you is equipped to conquer any challenge and seize the opportunities that await in the world of business

Also by Dr. Jose A. Mendez

Warrior Mindset: A Veteran's Guide to Entrepreneurship and Business
Next in Line: Navigating the World of Replaceability in Business

About the Author

Dr. Jose A. Mendez is not your average author; he's a man of unwavering faith, a loving husband, Air Force veteran, father, and ardent dog lover, especially his service dog Knox, a Black Labrador who is his faithful companion. Dr. Mendez is a multifaceted professional whose journey through life has been as diverse as it is inspiring.

Born and raised in the vibrant West Coast of Puerto Rico, Dr. Mendez's early life was deeply influenced by his cultural heritage and the stunning natural beauty of his island home. It's here that he developed a lifelong passion for outdoor adventures, particularly scuba diving, kayaking, and fishing.

Dr. Mendez's commitment to faith is the result of a life-changing experience; and has been a guiding force throughout his life. As a man deeply rooted in Christian principles, he has applied his unwavering belief system to every facet of his personal and professional life. His faith is the cornerstone upon which he has built his career as an educator, author, and entrepreneur.

With an impressive educational background, Dr. Mendez holds a Doctorate in Business Administration with specializations in Entrepreneurship and Business Management. He has also earned a Master's degree in Business Administration with a focus on Project Management and Quality Control, showcasing his commitment to excellence and precision in every endeavor.

Dr. Mendez's journey has also been marked by his dedication to service. He is a military veteran, having proudly served his country. His time in the military has not only enriched his character but has instilled in him a profound sense of duty, discipline, and leadership. As well as giving him a deep understanding of the best and worst that humanity has to offer.

Beyond his academic and professional achievements, Dr. Mendez is a devoted family man. As a loving husband and father, he cherishes the bonds he shares with his loved ones and draws inspiration from their unwavering support.

In his latest work, "Warrior Mindset: A Veteran's Guide to Entrepreneurship and Business," Dr. Mendez combines his expertise in business with his understanding of the military warrior mindset, to offer readers a unique perspective on how to build successful, purpose-driven businesses.

About the Publisher

At Christian Cross Publishing, we believe in the power of stories. Our vision is aimed at empowering faith through literature. We strive to illuminate hearts and minds with inspirational words that embody the timeless message of love, hope, and redemption.

Read more at https://christiancrosspublishing.com/.